SMART BRAIN RIGHT BRAIN

Exploring Our Earth

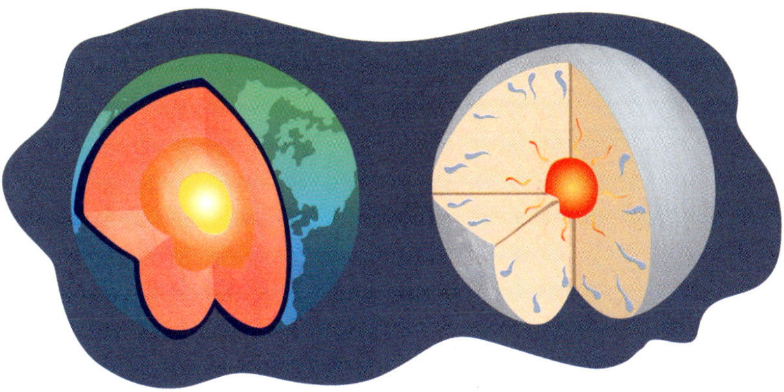

Om KIDZ
An imprint of Om Books International

First Published in 2021 by

Om KIDZ | Om Books International

Corporate & Editorial Office
A-12, Sector 64, Noida 201 301
Uttar Pradesh, India
Phone: +91 120 477 4100
Email: editorial@ombooks.com
Website: www.ombooksinternational.com

Sales Office
107, Ansari Road, Darya Ganj
New Delhi 110 002, India
Phone: +91 11 4000 9000
Email: sales@ombooks.com

Author: Shweta Sinha
Editor: Kirti Pathak
Art & Design: Anshuman Pandey, Gaurav Bhandari, Harish Arya

ISBN: 978-93-5276-835-6

Printed in India

10 9 8 7 6 5 4 3 2 1

CONTENTS

1. The Story of Earth

From space, Earth looks like a magnificent blue and white marble. It is due to an abundance of water and atmosphere. Hence Earth is also called the 'Blue Planet'. But Earth wasn't always like this.

How did Earth begin?

About 4.5 billion years ago (BYA) Earth was too hot to support life as there was no air or water.

Young Earth was mostly molten. This caused heavy metals, like liquid iron, to sink towards the centre. There they concentrated and formed the hot metallic core. The less dense silicate liquids settled on top. This separation of liquid metal elements is known as the 'Iron Catastrophe'.

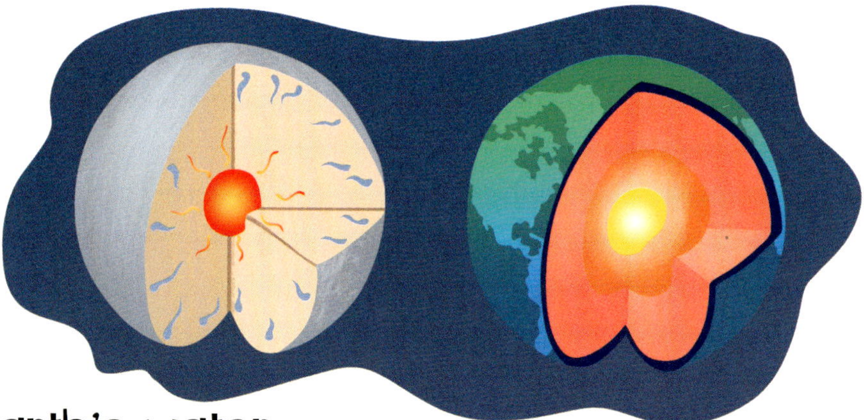

Earth's water

Earth was constantly hit by meteors, comets and asteroids. This created volcanoes on the surface. Water vapour and gases trapped inside rocks were forced out through the volcanoes and formed Earth's atmosphere.

Around 3.8 BYA, the water vapour condensed and it rained for almost 1,000 years. This, along with the ice-rich comets bombarding the Earth, helped cool down the planet and gave it all of its water. We now had our oceans.

Life on Earth

The temperature on Earth is just right for water—neither too hot to boil it away, nor too cold to freeze it. Our atmosphere too has lots of oxygen, which is much needed for life.

Around 3.5 BYA, Earth had finally cooled down. But underneath the upper layers of Earth was still a sea of molten liquids. The land masses drifted on them and collided with each other. About 600 million years ago, the Earth's surface reshaped itself to form the supercontinent—Pangaea.

While fossils suggest that some life-forms emerged about 3.5 BYA, the age of dinosaurs came much, much later.

The first animals

The first animals lived inside dark oceans and had simple, leaf-shaped bodies. They were rooted to the seabed and derived their food from the water. These creatures had no head, legs, arms, senses or internal organs.

DID YOU KNOW?

The fossil of Charnia, the first animal on Earth, was first found by a schoolboy in England in 1957!

Charnia - the first animal on Earth

A timeline of Earth's history

Earth has been around for 4.54 billion years. If we could compress this history into a 24-hour clock, this is how it would look:

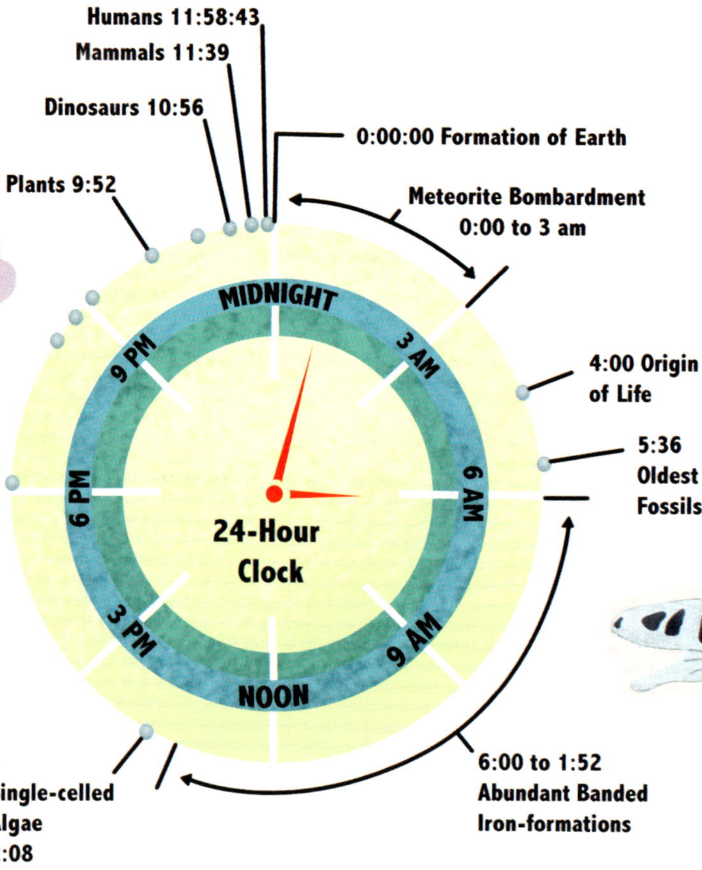

Humans arrive at 11:58 pm. If Earth has been in existence for only 24 hours, then all of our human history has lasted only two minutes.

POCKET FACT

Earth gained much of its ozone layer and became oxygen-rich only after the process of photosynthesis began to occur in plants.

2. Journey to the Centre of the Earth

In a Jules Verne's book, Professor Lidenbrock travelled to the centre of the Earth. If you could go with him, what would you find? A world within a world with petrified trees, giant mushrooms and early humans? No. In fact you would discover a solid iron ball at the centre. And that Earth is layered inside, just like an onion.

The structure of Earth

The iron catastrophe event created three layers inside Earth: Crust, Mantle and Core.

Crust

The crust is the solid outermost layer on which we live. It is at least 40 km deep. Land, or the 'continental crust', is made mostly of granite rock. The oceanic crust makes the ocean floor and covers two-thirds of Earth's surface. Mainly made of a hard rock called basalt, it is 8 km deep.

DID YOU KNOW?

In his 1864 novel, 'A Journey to the Center of the Earth', Jules Verne describes the centre of Earth as a hollow space—a theory popular in Europe at the time.

Mantle

Underneath the crust is the mantle, which is the largest and the heaviest layer. It is made of molten iron, minerals and semi-solid rocks. The thick rock in the sea floor presses into the mantle.

Core

The core is the centre of Earth where the heavy metals are concentrated. It has two layers—inner and outer.

The **outer core** contains liquid iron and nickel as well as sulphur and oxygen. It is super hot with temperatures from 4,000°C to 6,000°C. As Earth rotates, the outer core spins and generates Earth's magnetic field.

The **inner core** is made mainly of iron and is as hot as the Sun's surface! Yet, it is solid due to the high pressures surrounding it.

Tectonic Plate

Tectonic plates are a combination of Earth's crust and mantle. They fit together like a jigsaw puzzle to form Earth's surface. The plates are in constant movement. When they bump into each other at the fault lines, we feel the ground shake. That's an earthquake.

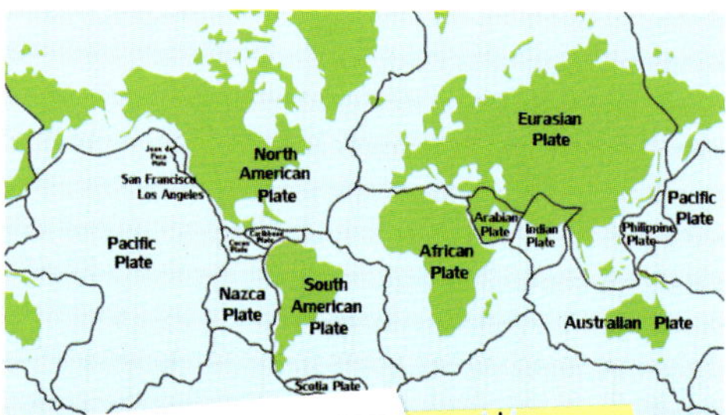

POCKET FACT

Geologists have learned about Earth's structure by studying the seismic waves generated by earthquakes and the movement of oceans.

3. Activity: Layers of Earth

Let us create a 3-D model of the layers of Earth. You will need:

- 4 colours of modelling clay or play dough
- Dental floss.

1. Choose a colour to represent each of the layers: Crust, Mantle, Outer Core, Inner Core.

2. Take a little clay for the inner core and roll it into a ball.

3. Now roll out a thick disc of another colour and wrap it around the ball. Press gently else the colours may blend into each other. This is your outer core.

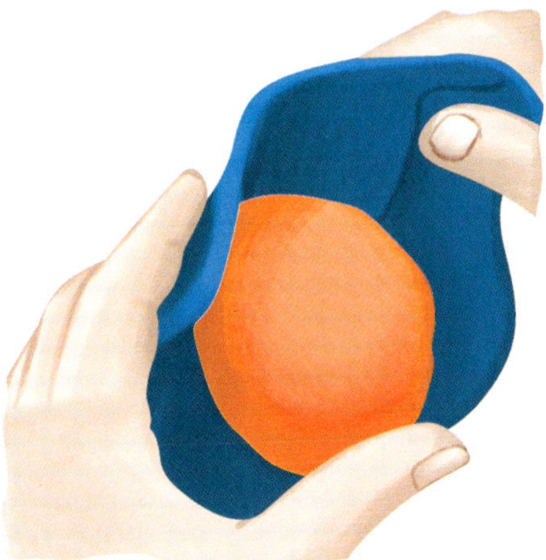

4. Similarly roll out the colour meant for the mantle and wrap it over your ball. Note that you will need more clay for every subsequent layer.

5. Repeat one more time to make the crust.

6. Once all your layers are done, use a piece of dental floss to gently cut the ball into half. You can now clearly see all the layers of your model Earth.

DID YOU KNOW?

If you could dig a tunnel right through the Earth and jump in, you would take 42 minutes and 12 seconds to reach the other side.

4. Rock vs. Mineral

Rocks are naturally occurring solids made of minerals clumped together. They can be hard and rigid or soft and crumbly. What kind of rocks do you find in your backyard?

Igneous Rocks

Lava is molten rock (magma) thrown out of a volcano. What happens when lava cools down and solidifies? It forms 'Igneous rocks', such as basalt. At times, bubbles mix with the magma, giving us light-weight, porous rocks called 'pumice'. Sometimes the solidification occurs underground. Granite is an underground rock.

Sedimentary Rocks

Look at this rock. See those lines? They are called strata. They indicate different sediment layers. The layers formed when sand, mud and pebbles were carried away by wind and water, and got deposited on top of each other. When the sediments were squashed together under high pressure, they formed sedimentary rocks. Often skeletons of animals and plants get buried with the sediments and form fossils.

Metamorphic Rocks

Metamorphic rocks form when igneous or sedimentary rocks change under intense heat or pressure, or both. They are generally found inside Earth's crust. Marble is a type of metamorphic rock that started out as sandstone, a sedimentary rock.

POCKET FACT

Uluru or Ayers rock, the famous monolithic rock in Australia, is a 500 million-year-old sedimentary rock.

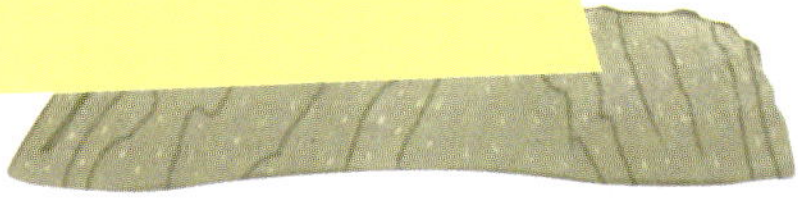

The Rock Cycle

Rocks are in a constant cycle, changing from one type to another over long periods of time and this cycle is endless.

Here is how this cycle works:

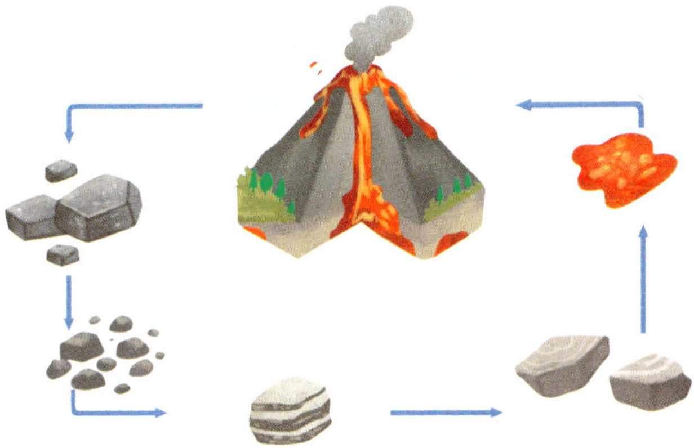

- Magma bursts through volcanoes, and solidifies to form igneous rocks.
- Wind, rain and snow erode rocks to form tiny pieces or sediments.
- These sediments are carried away by glaciers and rivers, breaking them further. They reach the sea where they settle at the bottom. High pressure pounds the sediment layers to harden and form sedimentary rocks.
- Heat and pressure deep underground change the buried rocks into metamorphic rocks.
- Underground rocks get heated and melt to form magma. The magma is thrown out of volcanoes, starting the cycle all over again.

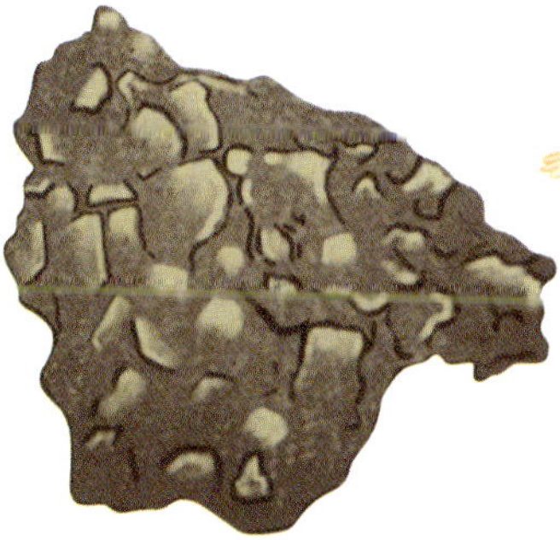

DID YOU KNOW?

Rocks from space sometimes land on Earth. They are called meteorites.

What are Minerals?

Minerals are solids that occur naturally. They are inorganic, meaning they don't come from plants or animals. And they are made of chemicals. Minerals sound mysterious, don't they? What if you found out that minerals are all around you? Gold, silver, iron, copper, diamonds—all are minerals we commonly hear of.

Minerals bind together to form rocks. However, while minerals have a consistent chemical structure, rocks can contain more than one mineral.

Metals from Rocks

Rocks that contain metals as minerals are called ores. Sometimes ores are easily available near Earth's surface. At other times we need to dig several feet underneath. Heat and chemicals are used to melt the ore and separate it from the pure metal. Gold, silver and copper are found in their pure form in ores.

DID YOU KNOW?

There are 4,000 different minerals on our planet!

5. Landforms

A continent is a large, solid area of land. Our world has seven continents—Asia, Europe, North America, South America, Africa, Australasia and Antarctica. Each continent has a wide range of landforms. Landforms are names given to the shapes of land around us.

Mountain

Mountains are tall pieces of land with steep sides. The top of a mountain is its peak or summit. Weather there can change without a warning. The base is where the mountain meets regular land. Valleys are low lying areas between mountains. Mountains occur in groups called ranges. One-fifth of Earth's land is covered with mountain ranges. Spot all the mountain ranges of the world:

Mountains are of different types—fold, dome, block and volcanic mountains. Fold mountains are the most common type of mountains across the world. They form when two tectonic plates collide against each other, forcing the crust to push upwards and fold.

POCKET FACT

The longest mountain range on land is the Andes. The Andes range runs 7,200 km along the western edge of South America.

6. Activity: Making Fold Mountains

You need: Towels, two boxes.

1. Fold the towels in half and stack them on the floor.

2. Place a box on each side of the towels.

3. Push the two boxes towards each other. Can you guess what will happen?

Watch the towels in between the boxes as they crumple and fold. This is how 'fold mountains' form when continental plates push against each other.

DID YOU KNOW?

Mount Everest may be the tallest mountain on land, but there are mountains under the sea that are taller than Everest.

Plateau

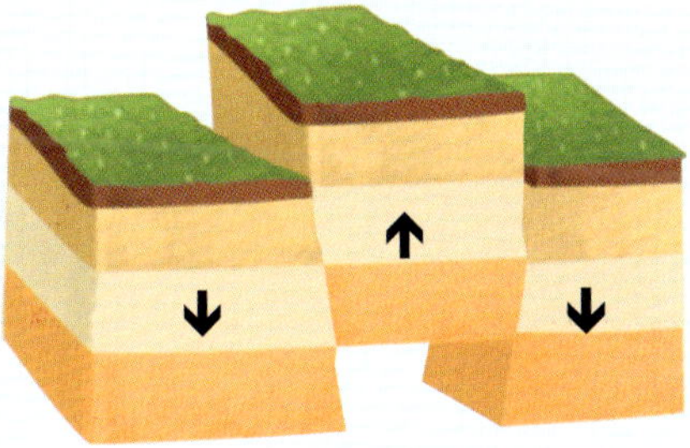

Block Mountain and Plateaus

A plateau is essentially a flat piece of land in high places and is often surrounded by mountains. The Tibetan plateau in the Himalayas is the highest and the largest plateau in the world. Plateaus often form alongside 'Block mountains'. Blocks of Earth drop next to each other to form a high mountain and a lower plateau.

Island

An island is a piece of land surrounded by water. Islands occur in oceans, seas, lakes or rivers. A group of islands is called an archipelago. The Japanese archipelago consists of four large islands and more than 3,000 smaller islands.

Islands are of two types—Oceanic and Continental. Oceanic islands were formed by volcanoes erupting from the sea floor. The Hawaiian islands are oceanic islands and are still being formed. Continental islands are a part of a main continental land but are now separated by a stretch of water. Greenland, the world's largest island, is separated from North America by a shallow sea.

POCKET FACT

Climate change is raising sea levels and threatening to submerge several small islands that dot our oceans.

Plain

Plains are flat, open lands. They exist on all continents except Antarctica and occupy one-third of Earth's land. Plains usually have a fertile soil and are used as farmlands. Land transportation is effortless and rivers are also easier to navigate, as plains offer fewer obstacles. As a result, more human settlements have been built on plains than at any other place.

Desert

A desert is a dry, arid region which can be extremely hot during the day and freezing cold at night. Deserts are either hot, cold or coastal. The Sahara is a hot desert, the Gobi is a cold desert while the Atacama is a coastal desert. All deserts have extremely low rainfall, hardly any plants or animals, and strong winds.

What do you imagine when you think of a desert? Lots and lots of sand, isn't it? But not all deserts are like that. Some have flat, stony grounds, others are covered with rocky hills. An oasis is a small pocket of vegetation in a desert where underground water is available. The water in some oases is from rain that fell 20,000 years ago.

POCKET FACT

The driest place on Earth is the Atacama desert in Chile. It may not receive any rainfall for several years.

Ocean and Sea

The five oceans – the Pacific, Atlantic, Indian, Arctic and Southern – are actually interconnected to form one single large water body. Each ocean may have its own currents, but water constantly flows from one to the other. A smaller area of water close to land is called a sea. Two-thirds of Earth's surface is covered with salty water.

Coastal Area

A coast is a strip of land bordering a sea or an ocean. Coasts have some of the most interesting land features, including beaches, salt marshes, deltas, lagoons, cliffs and caves. Tides, waves and water currents have carved out these coastal features over thousands of years.

Cliffs form where high land meets the sea. Powerful waves constantly batter the coast with such force that it shatters solid rock. This constant weathering carves out steep-sided cliffs and sea caves. The broken pieces of rock are carried away to more sheltered and calmer coastlines, where they form sandy beaches, pebble banks and mudflats.

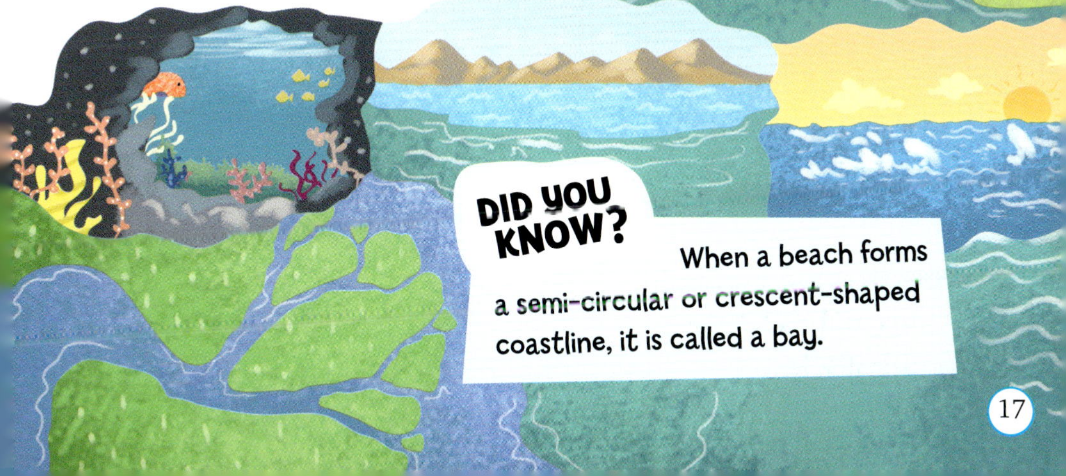

DID YOU KNOW?

When a beach forms a semi-circular or crescent-shaped coastline, it is called a bay.

7. Volcano

Any hole on the Earth's surface through which molten rock or magma can break through is a volcano.

Volcanoes can be active, dormant or extinct. An active volcano is one that has erupted at least once in recorded history. A dormant one has not erupted in recorded history, but can erupt again. An extinct volcano will never erupt again.

How does a volcano erupt?

Magma lies deep under Earth's crust. It rises up the gaps in the crust and collects in an area called a magma chamber. As the chamber fills up, pressure begins to build. The pressure pushes the magma up a pipe-like vent to Earth's surface. If the pressure is high, the eruption blasts magma into the air as ash, dust and rocks (volcanic bombs). At other times, magma flows on the surface as a hot, bright orange liquid called lava.

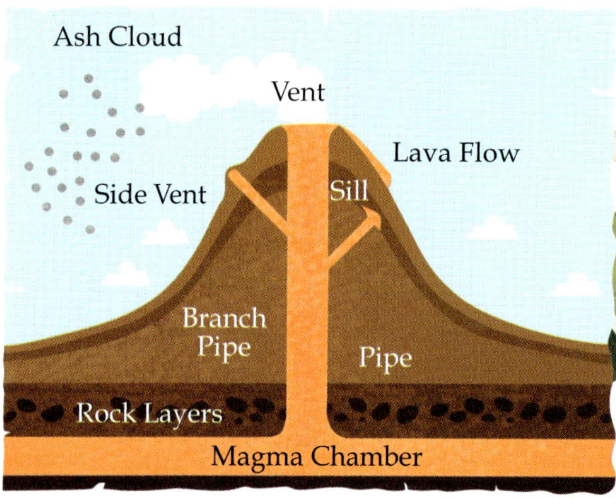

POCKET FACT

A volcano on the island of Stromboli, Italy, has been erupting almost continuously for the past 2,000 years.

Where are volcanoes located?

Volcanoes lie close to the boundary of Earth's tectonic plates. Not all volcanoes are visible on the ground. Several lie under the seas and oceans. In the Pacific Ocean lies a chain of volcanoes that together form a huge arc. This arc of volcanoes is called the Ring of Fire.

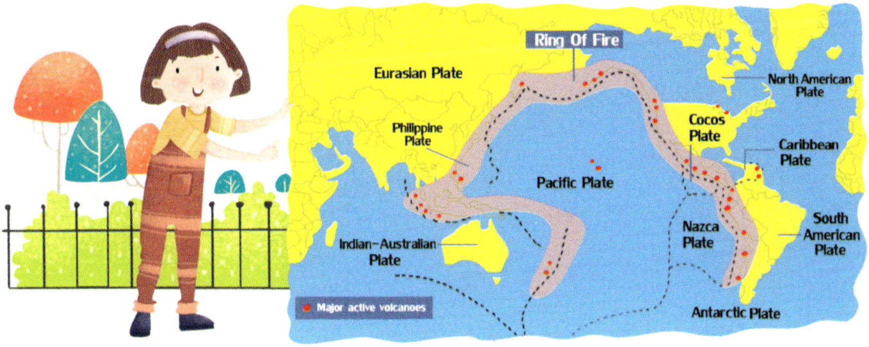

Hot Springs and Geysers

At times, tube-like holes filled with water run deep underground. Magma close to the bottom of the tube superheats the water to well above its boiling point. This boiling water turns into water vapour. As vapour tends to rise upwards, it shoots up the tube towards the surface. There, it erupts as hot springs or as jets of water and steam, called a geyser. After the eruption, water slowly seeps back into the tube and the process begins all over again.

At such high temperatures, the superheated water dissolves minerals from the underground rocks and brings them up to the hot springs. Mudpots form when the chemicals in water attack rocks, resulting in a bubbling, hot liquid mud.

DID YOU KNOW?

In Japan, monkeys called the Japanese macaque, dip themselves in hot springs to stay warm during freezing winters.

8. Activity: Let's Make a Volcano

You need:

- 10 ml dish soap
- 100 ml water
- 400 ml white vinegar
- Food colouring
- Baking soda slurry – Fill half a cup with baking soda and half with water and mix gently
- Empty 2-litre soda bottle, or a cup

Note: Go outside for this experiment, else you might end up with a lot of mess to clean up.

1. Mix the vinegar, dish soap and two drops of food colouring in the bottle.
2. Place the bottle on the floor. To keep it steady, you can build a small mound with mud or pebbles around it. The mound will also give the look of a real volcano while keeping the bottle steady.
3. Make sure your baking soda slurry is properly mixed. Give it another stir just to be sure.
4. Pour the slurry in the bottle and step back quickly.

What happened here?

Baking soda reacts with vinegar to give off a gas called carbon dioxide. This is the same gas used in sodas. As there is not enough space in the bottle for the gas to spread out, it quickly leaves through the bottle opening, creating an eruption. Just like what happens when you try to shake a can of soda.

9. Earth's Atmosphere

Earth is enveloped in a layer of gases and water vapour that make up the atmosphere. The atmosphere provides us with air, moisture, warmth, and protects us from the harmful rays of the Sun. Earth's atmosphere is made of layers, too.

Troposphere

The lowermost layer is the 'troposphere'. This is where we live and breathe. It contains mainly nitrogen and oxygen gases. The troposphere is about 16 km high from the surface of Earth. Weather is created here by the Sun's heat. Aircrafts fly at the very top of troposphere. The air gets thinner and colder as you go higher up. Beyond 8,000 meters, humans need special equipment to breathe. This is why mountaineers carry oxygen cylinders to Mount Everest, which is 8,848 m tall.

Stratosphere

The stratosphere lies above the troposphere and stretches up to 50 km from the surface of the Earth. This layer contains a key element necessary for our survival - the ozone layer. Ozone is an important gas that absorbs the harmful UV rays from the Sun and keeps us safe. Unfortunately, air pollution is damaging this layer and depleting it steadily.

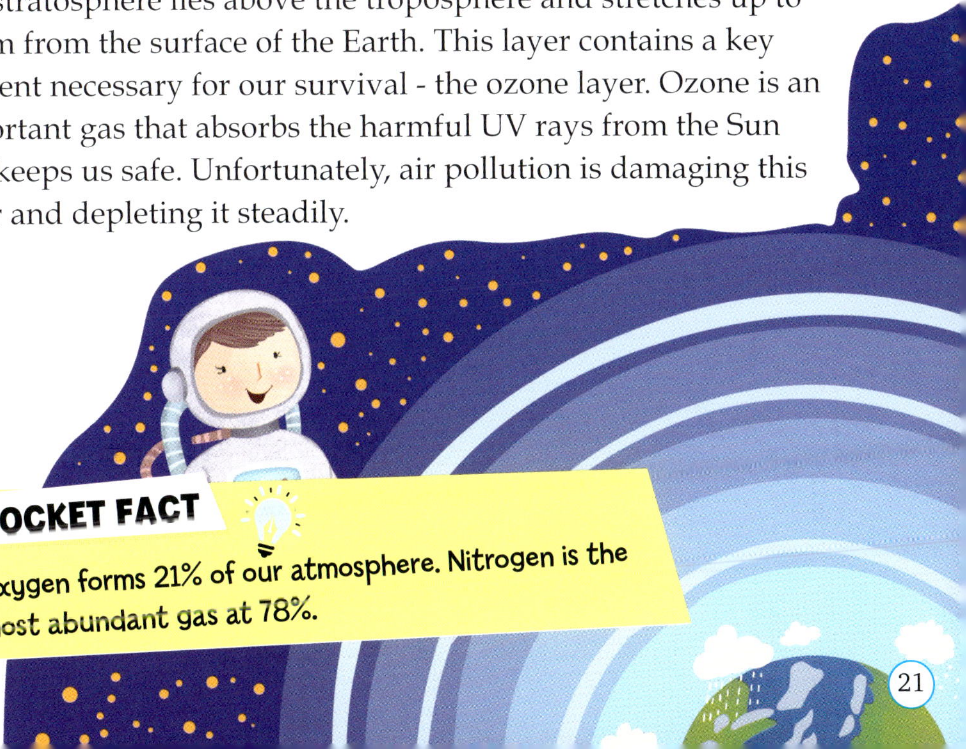

POCKET FACT

Oxygen forms 21% of our atmosphere. Nitrogen is the most abundant gas at 78%.

Mesosphere

Mesosphere lies between 50-80 km from Earth's surface. The air at the top of this layer is a bitter –143^{0} C. This is colder than anywhere else on the planet. Meteors entering our atmosphere generally burn up in the mesosphere, creating shooting stars.

Thermosphere

Beyond mesosphere, it only gets hotter and hotter. The thermosphere stretches from 80 km to about 600 km from Earth. The thermosphere absorbs the Sun's rays and can get as hot as 2000^{0} C. Auroras or Northern Lights are a spectacular show of multi-coloured, dancing lights, visible near the poles. Auroras are created in the thermosphere when particles from the Sun are drawn into it.

Exosphere

Beyond the thermosphere, lies the exosphere. This layer has no clear boundaries. The atmosphere gradually merges into space with only wisps of gas floating around.

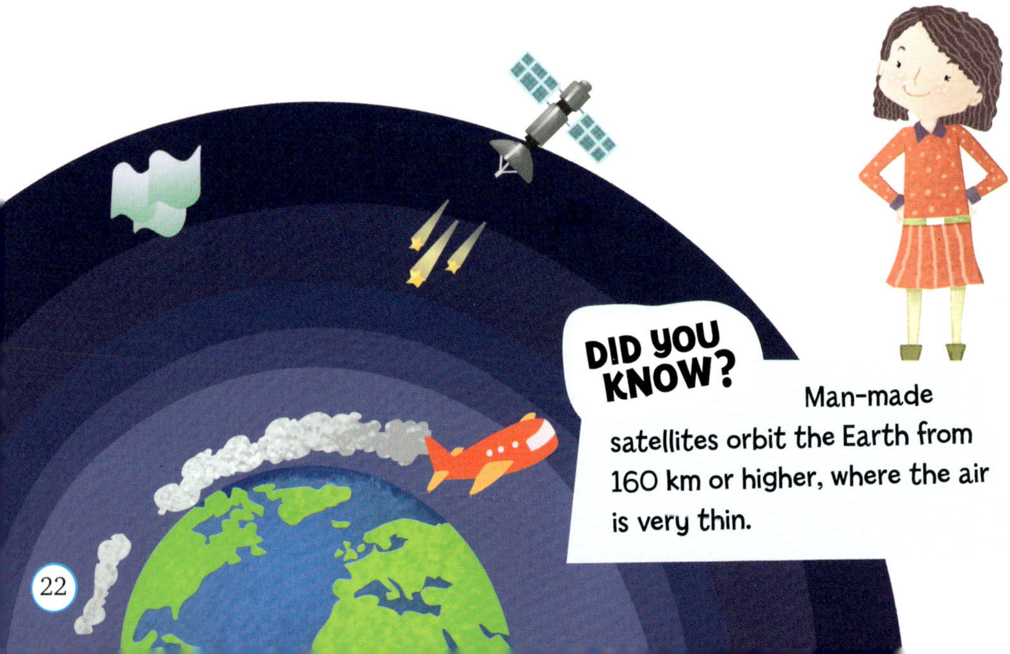

DID YOU KNOW?

Man-made satellites orbit the Earth from 160 km or higher, where the air is very thin.

10. Weather

Weather is how you would describe the sky and air outside, like windy or cloudy. It influences your day-to-day routine. A cold day will make you pull out a jacket. A storm may force you indoors.

What causes weather?

Weather is influenced by the Sun's energy and our planet's tilt on its axis. Places close to the equator receive more heat from the Sun than those near the poles. This warms the air to different temperatures at different places. As warm air rises, cooler air rushes in to take its place. This movement of air causes winds.

Winds change weather. They may bring in heavy rain or blow away the cloud cover. Moisture in the air influences weather too. It dictates how clouds form and whether it will rain, snow or produce a fog.

Types of weather

We experience different types of weather like rain, snow, thunderstorms, hot and sunny, etc. Various factors influence weather, including our location and the landforms around us. Places on the equator may be hot, but on a mountain, temperatures tend to be low even at the equator.

POCKET FACT

The weather pattern a region sees over a year defines its climate. Climate can be Tropical, Desert, Sub-tropical, Continental or Polar.

Rain

Clouds form when the Sun's heat evaporates water from oceans, seas, lakes and rivers. Warm air naturally rises, carrying the water vapour up in the atmosphere, where the vapour combines to form clouds. As the vapour rises, it meets cool air and changes back into water drops. Water drops combine to form bigger droplets, which then fall back on the Earth as rain.

This process is called the **Water Cycle**.

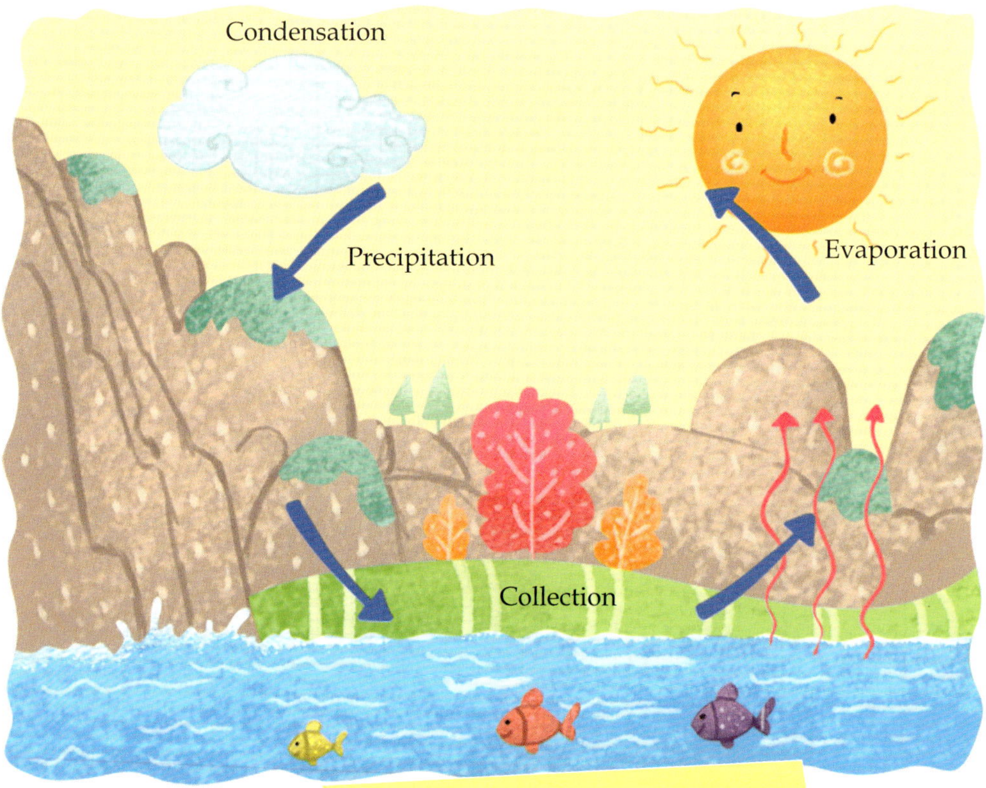

POCKET FACT

Earth does not make any new water. It has been recycling its water for over 4 billion years.

Snow

Clouds are full of water droplets that fall on the Earth as rain. However, if the temperature in the cloud is below freezing point, water droplets turn into ice crystals and fall as snow.

Thunderstorm

Heavy rain accompanied by thunder and lightning is called a thunderstorm. Lightning are bright flashes in the sky, created by a build-up of static electricity in the clouds. The thunder that follows is caused by the heat generated by the lightning flash. The heat greatly raises the temperature of air and causes it to expand suddenly. The noise we hear is the sound of this sudden expansion.

DID YOU KNOW?

The rolling sound of thunder we hear is due to echoes from the ground, mountains and hills or from buildings.

Hurricane

Also called typhoons or cyclones, hurricanes are tropical storms that build up over warm oceans. If they reach land, they leave a trail of destruction. The wind in a hurricane blows in a circle, like a spinning top. An area of calmer weather lies in the centre, known as the 'Eye of the Storm'. Hurricanes even whip up huge waves causing sudden flooding of coastal areas.

Tornado

Tornadoes are another type of violent windstorms where air whirls upwards rapidly. Another name for a tornado is 'twister'. No one exactly knows what causes a tornado but it frequently occurs when colder air from high up meets warmer air or wind lower down. Unlike hurricanes, tornadoes form on land. A tornado is grey in colour and resembles an elephant's trunk swaying down from the clouds to touch the ground. Tornadoes are most common in the southern states of the USA.

DID YOU KNOW?

Hurricanes have even been seen and photographed from space.

Tornado

11. Weather Forecasting

A farmer who grows crops is dependent on the weather for a good harvest. Airlines need to know the weather to schedule their flights. Weather forecasting helps issue timely warning in case of an approaching storm. Knowing how the weather will be helps you decide whether to take your snow boots or an umbrella.

How is weather forecasting done?

Today's weathermen use a number of equipments and observations to make accurate forecasts.

- Weather balloons filled with helium and hydrogen float in the atmosphere and send back useful weather information.
- Hundreds of weather satellites orbit Earth, constantly streaming photographs and data to us.
- Weather stations gather information using various equipments like barometers, thermometers and anemometers.

Do you want to predict the weather too?

Observe a pine cone. If its scales are closed , it means wet weather is coming your way.

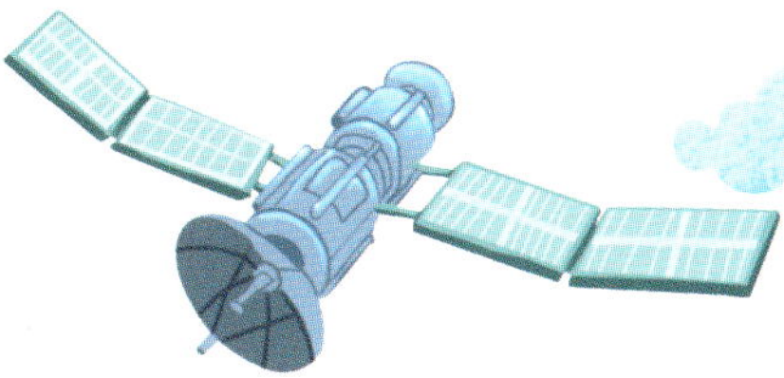

DID YOU KNOW?

Scientists who study the weather and make predictions are called Meteorologists.

Crossword

Solve the Crossword using the clues given:

Across

2. The outer layer of Earth.

5. The outermost layer of Earth's atmosphere.

7. The hot orange liquid a volcano spews out.

8. Rock that starts out as other types of rocks.

10. Gold, copper and diamond are types of ____.

11. Air that is moving from one place to another.

Down

1. A scientist who studies weather.

3. The name given to the lowest layer of Earth's atmosphere.

4. Himalayas are a type of _____ mountains.

5. When water changes to vapour.

6. Molten rock

9. Another name for a hurricane.

Mountain Ranges

Label the mountain ranges of the world.

Rockies	Andes	Alps
Himalayas	Great Dividing Range	

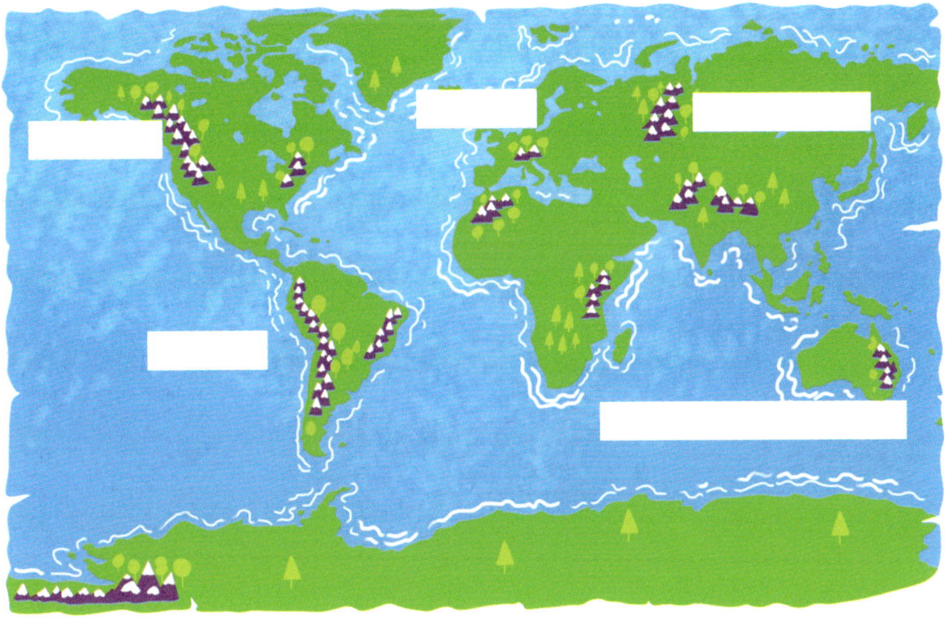

Fill in the blanks:

Complete the statements below with the correct answer:

1. The two elements that make up Earth's core are __________ and __________.
2. The inner core is as hot as the __________________.
3. Marble is a ___________ rock that derives from _____________.
4. A rock that contains a metal is called an ______.
5. _________ is a light-weight, porous rock that can float on water.
6. Sedimentary rocks have layers called __________.
7. A rock from space that lands on Earth is a ____________.
8. Deserts can be ______, _______ or __________.
9. ______________ are huge slabs in Earth's crust that fit like a jigsaw puzzle.
10. ______________ and ____________ are violent storms that are types of extreme weather.

Know your planet:

State whether true or false:

1. Earth was formed 4.5 billion years ago. (True/False)
2. The centre of Earth is hollow. (True/False)
3. The solid layer that we live on is called the 'Mantle'. (True/False)
4. A plateau is a flat-topped hill. (True/False)
5. Hurricanes form over land and tornados form over water. (True/False)
6. Several volcanoes exist under water and are hidden from us. (True/False)
7. A snowstorm with high speed winds causes blizzards. (True/False)
8. Cyclones can cause coastal areas to get flooded by sea water. (True/False)
9. Fault lines are where the tectonic plates touch each other. (True/False)
10. Minerals come from plants. (True/False)

GLOSSARY

Abundance	a lot of
Anemometer	tool to measure wind speed
Arid	having little or no rain
Barometer	tool to measure air pressure
Chemical	a substance that cannot be broken down without changing it into something else, e.g., water and oxygen
Crystal	a solid that has a regularly repeating internal arrangement of its atoms
Element	a pure substance that are the building blocks for all the rest of the matter in the world
Extreme	existing in a very high degree
Forecasting	a prediction about how something (as the weather) will develop
Geologist	scientists who study the physical features and history of Earth
Photosynthesis	the process in which green plants use sunlight to make their own food
Thermometer	tool to measure temperature
Weather station	a facility with tools and technology used to forecast the weather

ANSWERS

Page 28.

Page 29.

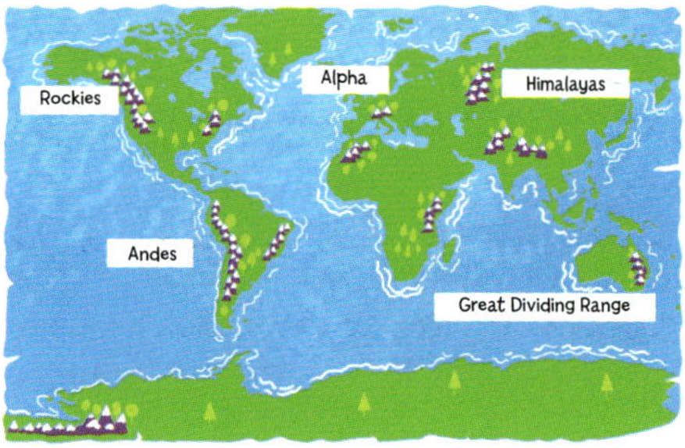

Page 30. 1. iron, nickel 2. surface of the Sun
3. metamorphic, sandstone 4. ore
5. Pumice 6. strata 7. meteorite
8. hot, cold, coastal 9. Tectonic Plates
10. Hurricanes, tornados

Page 31. 1. True 2. False
3. False 4. True
5. False 6. True
7. True 8. True
9. True 10. False